DEMCO

In the Footsteps of Explorers

Roald Amundsen
The Conquest of the South Pole

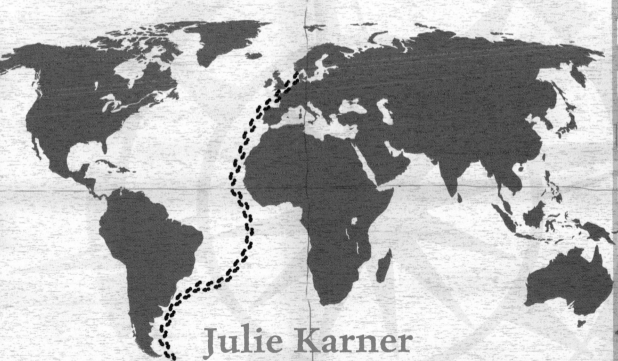

Julie Karner

Crabtree Publishing Company

www.crabtreebooks.com

Crabtree Publishing Company

www.crabtreebooks.com

Coordinating editor: Ellen Rodger
Series editor: Carrie Gleason
Editors: Rachel Eagen, Adrianna Morganelli, L. Michelle Nielsen
Design and production coordinator: Rosie Gowsell
Cover design and production assistance: Samara Parent
Art direction: Rob MacGregor
Scanning technician: Arlene Arch-Wilson
Photo research: Allison Napier

Photo Credits: Bibliotheque Nordique, Paris, France, Archives Charmet/The Bridgeman Art Library International: p. 20; Private Collection/The Bridgeman Art Library International: p. 19; Private Collection, The Stapleton Collection/The Bridgeman Art Library International: p. 5 (bottom), pp. 6-7, p. 22 (bottom), p. 23 (bottom); Bettmann/Corbis: cover, p. 10, p. 11, p. 16, p. 18, p. 24, p. 25, p. 27 (bottom), p. 28; Corbis: p. 7 (bottom), p. 13 (bottom), p. 17; Hulton-Deutsch Collection/Corbis: pp. 8-9 (both), p. 21; Chris Lisle/Corbis: p. 30; Galen Rowell/Corbis: p. 31 (top); Paul A. Souders/Corbis: pp. 12-13, p. 31 (bottom); Underwood & Underwood/Corbis: p. 29; Mary Evans Picture Library/The Image Works: p. 22 (top), p. 26; Ann Ronan Picture Library/HIP/The Image Works: p. 27 (top); SSPL/The Image Works: p. 15 (middle); Southern Illinois University/Photo Researchers, Inc.: p. 15 (top). Other images from stock CD.

Illustrations: Colin Mayne: p. 4

Cartography: Jim Chernishenko: title page, p. 19

Cover: Amundsen learned how to survive in sub-zero temperatures by following the examples set by the Inuit peoples of the Canadian Arctic. This included wearing a heavy fur parka, as shown in this picture.

Title page: Antarctica, home of the South Pole, is a continent covered with glaciers and ice.

Sidebar icon: Several species of penguin are native to Antarctica.

Library and Archives Canada Cataloguing in Publication

Karner, Julie, 1976-
   Roald Amundsen : the conquest of the South Pole / Julie Karner.

(In the footsteps of explorers)
Includes index.
ISBN-13: 978-0-7787-2432-2 (bound)
ISBN-10: 0-7787-2432-8 (bound)
ISBN-13: 978-0-7787-2468-1 (pbk)
ISBN-10: 0-7787-2468-9 (pbk)

   1. Amundsen, Roald, 1872-1928--Travel--Antarctica--Juvenile literature.
2. Antarctica--Discovery and exploration--Norwegian--Juvenile literature.
3. South Pole--Discovery and exploration--Norwegian--Juvenile literature.
I. Title. II. Series.

G850 1910 A68.K37 2006   j919.8'9   C2006-902858-3

Library of Congress Cataloging-in-Publication Data

Karner, Julie, 1976-
   Roald Amundsen : The Conquest of the South Pole / written by Julie Karner.
      p. cm. -- (In the footsteps of explorers)
   Includes index.
   ISBN-13: 978-0-7787-2432-2 (rlb)
   ISBN-10: 0-7787-2432-8 (rlb)
   ISBN-13: 978-0-7787-2468-1 (pbk)
   ISBN-10: 0-7787-2468-9 (pbk)
   1. Amundsen, Roald, 1872-1928--Travel--Antarctica--Juvenile literature. 2. Antarctica--
      Discovery and exploration--Norwegian--Juvenile literature. 3. South Pole--Discovery
      and exploration--Norwegian--Juvenile literature. I. Title. II. Series.
   G850 1912 .A48 K37 2006
   919.8'9--dc22
                                                                            2006016037

Crabtree Publishing Company

Published in Canada
Crabtree Publishing
616 Welland Ave.
St. Catharines, ON
L2M 5V6

Published in the United States
Crabtree Publishing
PMB16A
350 Fifth Ave., Suite 3308
New York, NY 10118

Published in the United Kingdom
Crabtree Publishing
White Cross Mills
High Town, Lancaster
LA1 4XS

Published in Australia
Crabtree Publishing
386 Mt. Alexander Rd.
Ascot Vale (Melbourne)
VIC 3032

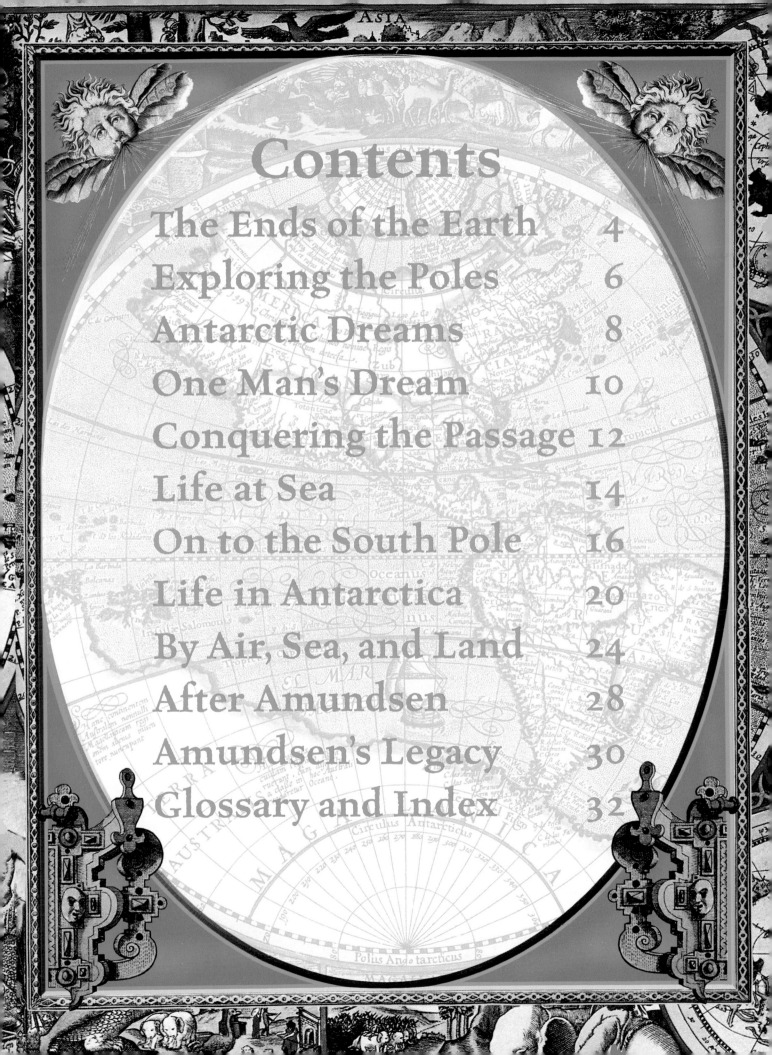

Contents

The Ends of the Earth

Roald Amundsen was a Norwegian adventurer who spent much of his life exploring the polar regions. He became famous for leading the first successful expedition to the South Pole. Amundsen's accomplishments and scientific discoveries at both ends of the Earth mark him as one of the most successful explorers of his time.

(above) Amundsen spent two years researching in the Arctic before becoming the first to navigate the Northwest Passage in 1905.

Gentlemen: To The Poles!

Amundsen lived at a time when the North and South poles were some of the last places on Earth to be explored by Europeans or North Americans. In the late 1800s and early 1900s, polar explorers were considered adventurous heroes who battled brutal weather, hunger, and ice to reach their goals. Polar expeditions were risky and required careful planning.

Pole to Pole

Like a handful of other explorers in the early 1900s, Amundsen spent years preparing for his ultimate goal of being the first to reach the North Pole. His dreams were dashed in 1909 when Americans Robert Peary and Matthew Henson, along with four Inuit guides, were the first to reach the North Pole. A disappointed Amundsen set his sights on Antarctica, home of the South Pole, instead. He became the first to reach the South Pole in 1911. Amundsen did not rest on his **laurels**. The South Pole **conquest**, followed by a flight over the North Pole in an **airship** in 1926, mark Amundsen as the first man ever to reach both poles.

Been There, Done That

Amundsen thrived on dangerous and challenging situations. He was inspired by tales of John Franklin, an early Arctic explorer who had been forced to eat shoe leather to avoid starvation. This led Amundsen into a life where he **endured** frostbite and blizzards, and suffered illness and hunger. Amundsen later spoke about his adventures on lecture tours and in journals detailing his expeditions. Here is what he said about his South Pole accomplishment:

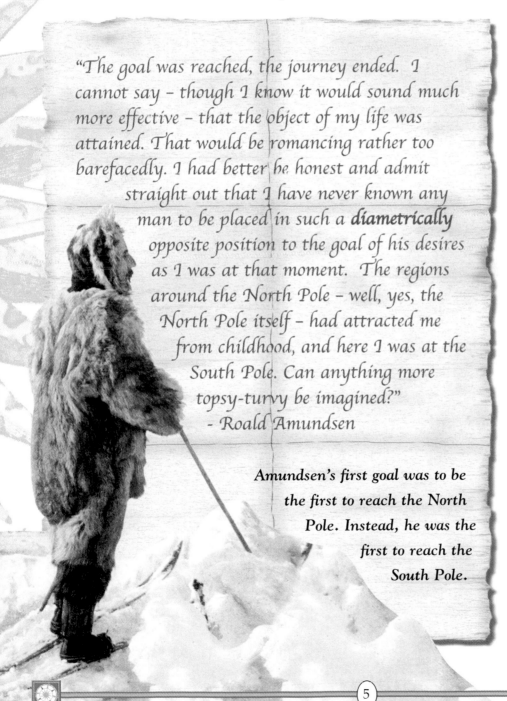

"The goal was reached, the journey ended. I cannot say – though I know it would sound much more effective – that the object of my life was attained. That would be romancing rather too barefacedly. I had better be honest and admit straight out that I have never known any man to be placed in such a **diametrically** opposite position to the goal of his desires as I was at that moment. The regions around the North Pole – well, yes, the North Pole itself – had attracted me from childhood, and here I was at the South Pole. Can anything more topsy-turvy be imagined?"
- Roald Amundsen

Amundsen's first goal was to be the first to reach the North Pole. Instead, he was the first to reach the South Pole.

- 1872 -

Amundsen is born in Borge, Norway.

- 1894 -

Amundsen first sets sail for the Arctic as a crew member on a sealing vessel.

- 1909 -

Robert Peary and Matthew Henson reach the North Pole.

- 1911 -

Amundsen's team raises the Norwegian flag at the South Pole.

Exploring the Poles

The golden age of exploration began in the 1400s, which was when Europeans sailed the seas in search of trade goods and wealth. By the late 1800s, explorers had visited and mapped most of the Earth's surface. The last frontiers of unknown territory lay in the Arctic and Antarctic regions.

The Northwest Passage

Around 1500, European countries charted sea routes around the southern coast of Africa to trade for spices in Asia. Shortly after, European sailors began searching for the Northwest Passage, a northern sea route from Europe to Asia. This route through the Arctic would shorten the journey and increase trade with the East. Many early European explorers who set sail in search of the Northwest Passage returned unsuccessful. Many others never returned.

(background) Explorers such as Amundsen learned how to survive in the frozen climates of the Arctic and Antarctic by adopting the fur clothing of the Arctic Inuit peoples.

Exploration and Adventure

In the late 1800s, the focus of world exploration was on the North and South poles. Explorers went in search of personal wealth, fame, and accomplishment, as well as **national glory**. Each explorer attempted to set a new record: to reach the farthest north, or to be the first to spend the winter in the Antarctic. Previous explorers had aimed for **practical** goals, such as land to inhabit, or resources, such as spices or furs, to **exploit**. The polar explorers pursued an idea. Even though the poles were just dots on a map, they represented huge accomplishments. Many men competed to be the first to plant their country's flag at the top or the bottom of the world.

Polar explorers from many countries vied to be the first to explore the poles. Here Amundsen, at left, congratulates American Admiral Richard E. Byrd for becoming the first to fly over the North Pole.

- 1558 -

John Davis searches for the Northwest Passage and names the Davis Strait, in Canada.

- 1576 -

Martin Frobisher names Frobisher Bay, near Baffin Island, while searching for the Northwest Passage.

- 1845 -

John Franklin and crew go missing on their search for the Northwest Passage.

Antarctic Dreams

British explorer and sea captain James Cook was the first to cross the Antarctic Circle in 1773. People had long assumed that there was a landmass at the bottom of the world, but Cook failed to spot land on his voyage.

Sightings of Land

Cook saw many whales, seals, and icebergs while sailing deep in the **Southern Hemisphere**. He did not sail far enough to sight land. Nearly 40 years later, further evidence of the Antarctic continent emerged. Many different explorers navigated Antarctic waters and mapped the coastline, contributing knowledge about the region. All reported huge stretches of ice that prevented ships from getting near land.

On the Continent

A Norwegian sealing and whaling vessel called the *Antarctic* made the first confirmed Antarctic landing in 1895. This led to other expeditions. One expedition was the first to spend a winter on the continent. Information on the plant and animal life of the area was collected.

James Cook's description of seals and whales in Antarctic waters prompted ships to travel to the area to hunt. Both seals and whales were in high demand for the oil extracted from their bodies, which was used in lamps. Whaling stations were set up on islands near the Antarctic until whale oil was replaced by other fuels.

Robert Scott

The Royal Society and the Royal Geographical Society of Great Britain were organizations that encouraged and granted money for scientific research. Both organizations helped fund a national expedition to Antarctica by naval captain Robert Falcon Scott in 1901. It was called the *Discovery* expedition. Its scientific aims were to accurately chart coastline and the land, and to make magnetic, physical, **geological**, and **biological observations**. Scott also wanted to be the first to reach the South Pole. He had no previous experience with polar conditions, and his party faced problems that forced them to end their search. Despite this, they discovered a route that led toward the South Pole and **trekked** farther south into the interior of the continent than anyone had previously.

Robert Scott set his sights again on the South Pole in 1910 with the Terra Nova expedition, named after his ship. Scott and four fellow explorers reached the pole shortly after Amundsen. The group died on the return trek after severe blizzards prevented them from traveling far and reaching their supply depots. His death was one of the greatest tragedies of polar exploration.

- 1773 -

James Cook determines Antarctica is a continent.

- 1819-1821 -

Russian captain Thaddeus Bellingshausen circumnavigates the Antarctic.

- 1821 -

American sealer John Davis lands on Antarctica.

- 1823 -

British whaler James Weddell names the Weddell Sea.

One Man's Dream

Roald Amundsen had one goal from the time he was a teenager: to be the first man to reach the North Pole. He read books, trained, and became an expert skier and a ship's captain. Even with these careful preparations, he could not prevent another explorer from reaching the North Pole first.

Growing Up

Amundsen was born into a wealthy ship-building family in southeast Norway. As a child, he was **captivated** by stories of polar exploration. He hoped to one day follow in the footsteps of those in the stories.

The tales of hardships faced by British explorer John Franklin fascinated Amundsen as a child. Franklin and his crew starved and froze to death while searching for the Northwest Passage.

Childhood Hero

The voyages of Norwegian explorer and scientist, Fridtjof Nansen, inspired Amundsen as a teenager. Nansen became famous in Norway when he trekked across Greenland in 1866. Nansen also planned an expedition to the North Pole and planted the Norwegian flag about 224 miles (360 kilometers) away from it, the northernmost point any European had reached to that date. Amundsen was determined to finish Nansen's journey.

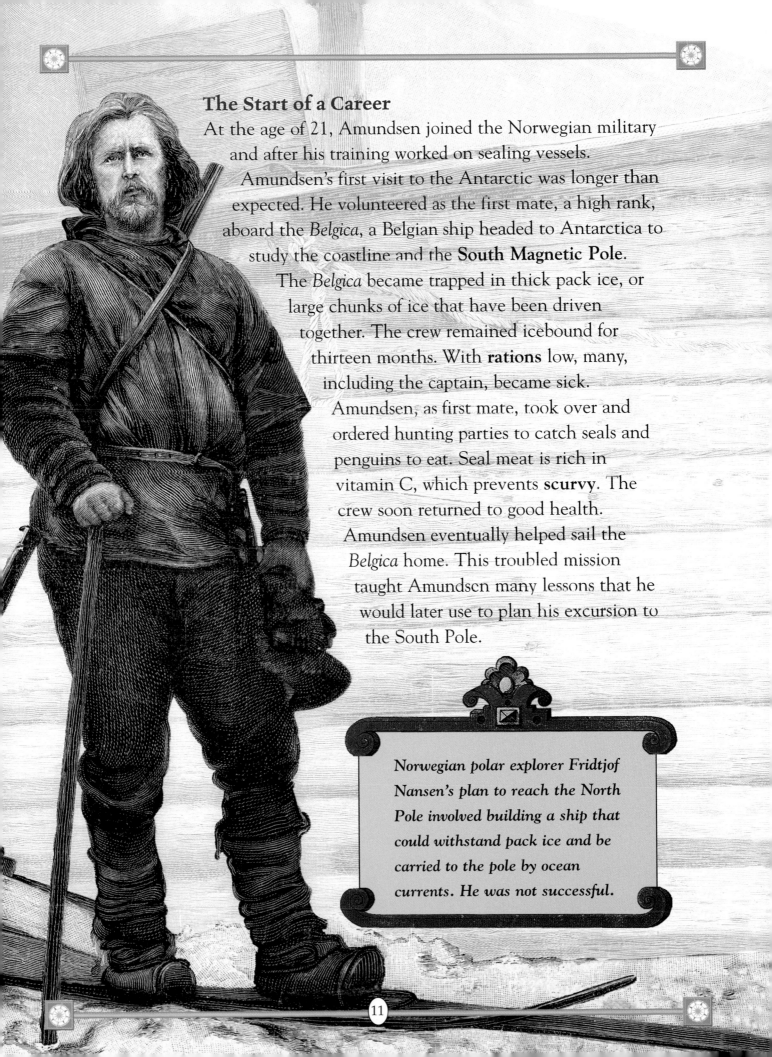

The Start of a Career

At the age of 21, Amundsen joined the Norwegian military and after his training worked on sealing vessels.

Amundsen's first visit to the Antarctic was longer than expected. He volunteered as the first mate, a high rank, aboard the *Belgica*, a Belgian ship headed to Antarctica to study the coastline and the **South Magnetic Pole**.

The *Belgica* became trapped in thick pack ice, or large chunks of ice that have been driven together. The crew remained icebound for thirteen months. With **rations** low, many, including the captain, became sick.

Amundsen, as first mate, took over and ordered hunting parties to catch seals and penguins to eat. Seal meat is rich in vitamin C, which prevents **scurvy**. The crew soon returned to good health.

Amundsen eventually helped sail the *Belgica* home. This troubled mission taught Amundsen many lessons that he would later use to plan his excursion to the South Pole.

Norwegian polar explorer Fridtjof Nansen's plan to reach the North Pole involved building a ship that could withstand pack ice and be carried to the pole by ocean currents. He was not successful.

Conquering the Passage

Amundsen was eager to lead a mission of his own to navigate the Northwest Passage. There was little commercial interest in the Northwest Passage by 1903, because the harsh weather and crushing ice was thought to make it too dangerous for a regular shipping route. Amundsen needed a scientific goal to receive financial support for his journey.

Pole Attraction

Amundsen's scientific goal was to study the **magnetic properties** in the area close to the **North Magnetic Pole**. The North Magnetic Pole had been discovered over 70 years before, but odd changes in compass readings over time suggested that the pole might not be stationary, or always in one place. Amundsen's mission was to set up a station along his Northwest Passage route to take precise magnetic readings. Amundsen purchased a small fishing ship called the *Gjoa* and stocked it with supplies and equipment for the journey. He was careful to stock the ship with ample food rations, since his earlier experience to Antarctica taught him it was impossible to predict how long a ship might be iced in, or how many years the voyage would take.

The Gjoa stopped in Greenland where it was loaded with more supplies including fish and meat for the men to eat, skis and sleds for overland travel, and Inuit dogs to pull the sleds. Today the ship is displayed at the Fram Museum in Oslo, Norway.

CJØA

Gjoahavn

The *Gjoa* found a safe port, which the crew named "*Gjoahavn*," which is present-day Gjoa Haven in Nunavut, Canada. Here the men set up camp for the next two years while they made magnetic observations. Their data showed that the North Magnetic Pole had moved 31 miles (50 kilometers) northward since its original discovery. This was the first proof that the North Magnetic Pole was not fixed in one place. As magnetic compasses relied on this pole for a reading of north, this was an important discovery.

Amundsen, front row far left, and the crew of the Gjoa. *The ship spent three years, from 1903 to 1906, in the Arctic.*

The Northwest Passage

By August 1905, Amundsen and the *Gjoa* had left *Gjoahavn* to journey west through the Northwest Passage. Navigating the passage was a nerve-racking experience. The water was deep one minute, and then dangerously shallow the next. Jagged rocks threatened to pierce the bottom of the ship, and the lead, a heavy piece of metal on a line, was continuously lowered into the water to check the depth. Since this was an uncharted route, there were many times when the *Gjoa* reached a dead end and had to retreat. In some spots, the ship had to force its way through icy passages by ramming ahead. After 14 days, they reached the Beaufort Sea at the western end of the Northwest Passage.

Life at Sea

Amundsen trained as a ship's captain, and early in his career served aboard a ship that spent more than a year in Antarctic waters. His experience prepared him for navigating the frozen seas at both poles.

The Ships

Amundsen used four ships and many crew in his explorations of the Northwest Passage in northern Canada and the South Pole in Antarctica. His first Antarctic experience was aboard the *Belgica* during the Belgian Antarctic Expedition of 1897 to 1899. The expedition was the first to winter in Antarctica when the *Belgica* became locked in ice. Crew members nearly starved and began suffering from scurvy, a disease caused by lack of vitamin C found in fresh vegetables and fruits.

(background) The hull of the Fram, *which Amundsen took to Antarctica, was made with thick wooden crossbeams reinforced with iron. The hull had a smooth, rounded shape that would allow it to slide upwards when ice pressed in on it from the sides. The* Fram's *cargo included a piano, a gramophone, a pet canary, and a library of 3,000 books.*

Ninety-seven husky sled dogs slept in kennels on the deck of the Fram, *for the 1910 to 1911 expedition to the South Pole.*

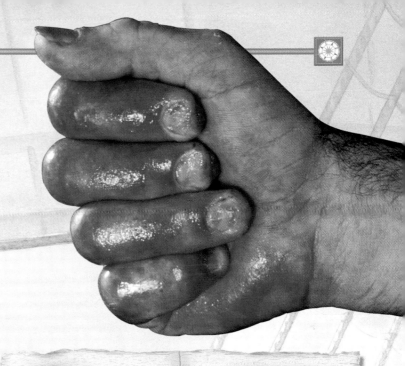

(right) Frostbite, a condition in which extremities, such as hands and feet, freeze, was always a danger. The Norwegian navy gave Amundsen 200 thick felt blankets to make into clothing for the 1910 expedition. The polar explorers also wore reindeer-skin clothing to keep warm.

(above) Medicine chests allowed explorers to carry needed medical supplies in a small container. The chests, which were new at the time, contained compressed tablets of medication in watertight cylinders.

(right) Cocoa was a welcome treat for polar explorers.

Hot Cocoa

Pemmican, or dried meat mixed with fat, as well as biscuits, chocolate, and powdered milk, were part of the daily rations of Amundsen's crew. Here is a modern recipe for hot cocoa, a drink enjoyed by Arctic and Antarctic explorers.

Ingredients:

2 cups (500 mL) powdered sugar
1 cup (250 mL) cocoa (Dutch-process preferred)
2 1/2 cups (625 mL) powdered milk
1 teaspoon (5 mL) salt
2 teaspoons (10 mL) cornstarch
  Boiling or hot water

  Directions:

  Mix ingredients. Use a kettle to boil water. Fill a mug halfway with the mixture and top with boiling water. Stir and enjoy.

On to the South Pole

After the success of the *Gjoa* mission, Roald Amundsen was ready to face a new and greater challenge. He prepared for his dream voyage to the North Pole. He did not know at the time that he would be planting the Norwegian flag at the South Pole rather than the North Pole.

To the North Pole!

Amundsen wanted to lead an expedition to the North Pole using Fridtjof Nansen's idea of allowing his ship to be frozen into the pack ice and drifting over the pole. He acquired Nansen's ship, the *Fram*, which was specially designed to withstand the crushing pack ice of the Arctic Ocean. He assembled a crew of 18 men and was in the middle of preparing for the voyage when he received the news that Americans Robert Peary and Matthew Henson had already reached the North Pole.

A New Plan

Amundsen did not give up on exploring and even led people to believe he would continue with his mission to the North Pole. He hatched a secret plan to reach the South Pole instead. Unlike the *Gjoa* expedition, which had a scientific goal, Amundsen's aim for the South Pole expedition was simple: to be the first there. British explorer Robert Scott's expedition was already in Antarctica at the time, preparing for their assault. Amundsen and Scott would be competing for the same goal.

Peary, Henson, and four Inuit guides reached the North Pole on April 6, 1909, while Amundsen was preparing to leave on his journey to the pole. Amundsen carried on with his plans, sailed out of Norway, and then told his crew that they were heading for the South Pole instead.

Different Strategies

Like Amundsen, Scott was a veteran of Antarctic travel. Using his knowledge of the weather and the writings of previous explorers, Amundsen decided to approach the pole from the Ross Sea, a route different from Scott's. The Ross Ice Shelf is a giant, constantly moving glacier stretching along the coast of the Ross Sea. Amundsen set up his base camp, called Framheim, on a rocky and stable area of the ice shelf, in the Bay of Whales.

Waiting for the Sun

Amundsen's crew spent months preparing for the trek to the pole and making scientific observations. Amundsen was a **stickler** for preparation. Expedition members laid out carefully marked cachets, or supply depots, at latitudes of 80°, 81°, and 82° south along the route. They constantly tested their equipment and made modifications. The intense cold, reaching -69° Fahrenheit (-56° Celsius) forced one team to return to Framheim. Two of the men had heels so badly frozen that it took nearly two months for them to recover. Amundsen, with only four others, again set out for the pole.

(background) Amundsen's ship, the Fram, *foreground, and Scott's ship, the* Terra Nova, *anchored off Antarctic pack ice in 1911. Both explorers vied for the same goal but only one made it back.*

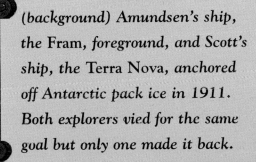

At Last, the Pole!

Amundsen and fellow Norwegians Oscar Wisting, Olav Bjaaland, Helmer Hanssen, and Sverre Hassel traveled on dog **sledges** for nearly two months. After passing a mountain range that Amundsen named the Queen Maud Mountains, the expedition killed 24 of the 42 dogs to lighten their load, and to feed themselves and the other dogs. On December 14, 1911, Amundsen reached his destination: a latitude of 90° south, or the South Pole. The men stayed at the pole for four days before making the return journey to Framheim in 13 days. The *Fram* was waiting for them, and the entire expedition sailed back to Norway.

(below) After taking measurements to prove they had reached the South Pole, the Amundsen expedition put up a tent, planted the Norwegian flag, and named the spot "Polheim," meaning home of the Pole. The tent contained a tablet bearing their names, a letter to Norway's King Haakon VII, and a letter to explorer Robert Scott who came across the tent weeks later. A disappointed and exhausted Scott and his team members were caught in blizzards and died on the return to their waiting ship.

Amundsen's expedition reached the South Pole and returned to their awaiting ship. Scott also reached the pole, but never made it back alive. This map shows their different routes and Scott's final camp, where he and his team died.

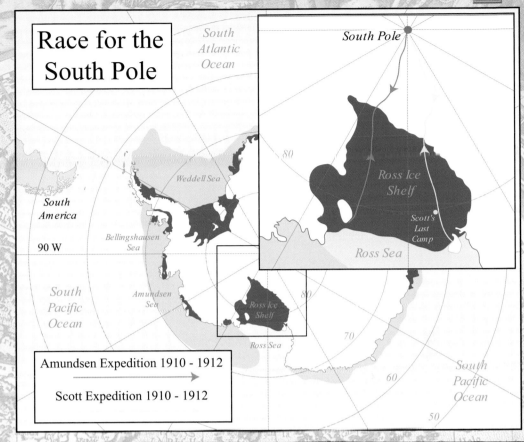

Race for the South Pole

South Atlantic Ocean

South Pole

80

Weddell Sea

South America

90 W

Bellingshausen Sea

South Pacific Ocean

Amundsen Sea

Ross Ice Shelf

Ross Sea

Ross Ice Shelf

Scott's Last Camp

Ross Sea

80

70

60

South Pacific Ocean

50

Amundsen Expedition 1910 - 1912 →

Scott Expedition 1910 - 1912

Shackleton in Antarctica

Amundsen had closely studied previous Antarctic expeditions, including British explorer Ernest Shackleton's 1907 to 1909 expedition. Shackleton took Manchurian ponies and a car on this expedition. The car seized up in the Antarctic cold and the ponies could not pull over crevices in the glaciers. Shackleton's team tried to haul the heavy sledges to the pole themselves. They came within 100 miles (160 kilometers) of their goal before they were forced to turn back.

Listen up penguins! Explorers brought some comforts with them.

Life in Antarctica

Even colder than the Arctic, Antarctica is a challenge for explorers. The only sources of food are the seals, penguins, and other birds that live in the coastal areas. Blizzards can produce winds of up to 200 miles per hour (320 kilometers per hour), and temperatures can dip as low as -129° Fahrenheit (-89° Celsius).

Framheim

Amundsen's base camp on Antarctica's Ross Ice Shelf was named Framheim. The camp consisted of a large, two-room wooden building for the men and another building containing a workroom, storeroom, washroom, and many tents to house supplies. The main building was constructed at Amundsen's home in Norway. It was taken down and labeled piece by piece so it could be set up again in Antarctica. The wind was so strong at Framheim that the roofs were fastened with steel wire to six long bolts driven into the ice to prevent the buildings from blowing away.

(background) The ice surrounding the Antarctic continent was a constant danger for ships. A ship could be frozen in, crushed, and sunk by the ice.

Framheim means "home of the Fram." The Fram brought Amundsen to the Antarctic and was home to the crew for several months.

Small Group

Amundsen knew from his experience on the *Belgica* expedition that too much time spent in the Antarctic with nothing to do would make the men unhappy and lead to fighting. To lead them through an unknown frozen land, he needed them to trust him. For this reason, he brought only a small crew. Of the nineteen men who had sailed to Antarctica on the *Fram*, only nine remained at Framheim to prepare for the polar excursion. The remaining crew sailed away aboard the *Fram* to spend the winter in Buenos Aires, Argentina.

During Amundsen's previous Arctic experience in the Northwest Passage, he used a number of instruments for polar navigation. Here he is shown using a sextant, an instrument that measures the angle between two objects. He also used a chronometer watch that measured the correct time of day, and an ancient method of exploration calculation called dead reckoning.

- 1910 -

Amundsen set sail in Fridtjof Nansen's ship, the *Fram*, designed especially for Arctic waters.

- December 16, 1911 -

Amundsen's team is the first to reach the South Pole.

- January 18, 1912 -

Robert Falcon Scott's team reaches the South Pole. Scott and five others die miles from their supply depot.

The sledges are unloaded at a supply cache. The stored food meant a lighter load going to the pole and coming back.

Keeping Busy

There was plenty of work to keep the men at Framheim busy. While the sled teams began depositing food at caches, the rest of the men built and stocked the camp. One of their tasks was to kill enough seals and penguins to supply them with meat for several months. The dark, stormy winter would prevent them from venturing out for food. During the winter, the most important task was preparing and perfecting their equipment for the trip to the pole. The goal was to make the sledges and provisions as light as possible to reduce the strain on the dogs and the men. In addition to this, there was the everyday work of maintaining the camp.

Amundsen was an excellent dog musher, or dogsledder. This helped him and his team reach the pole and return quickly.

To the Pole

The polar party faced frigid temperatures and fierce winds during their journey. While they were careful to dress in many lightweight layers of animal skins to keep warm, they still faced the risk of frostbite. They often had to rub the skin on their cheeks to keep them from freezing, and their faces suffered from painful sores from the frost for months afterward. They also trimmed their beards weekly to prevent thick layers of ice from forming in their facial hair.

Penguin meat provided protein needed to keep the crew members' muscles working.

The Daily Routine

Framheim ran like a workshop in the polar south. Amundsen believed that smaller groups were better than larger ones and routines helped keep people focused on a goal. The men had a regular routine of rising at 7:30 a.m., eating breakfast (below left), working from 9 a.m. until noon, eating lunch, and then working from 2 p.m. until 5:15 pm. Each man had specific duties. Two men were responsible for scientific observations. Carpenters (below right) prepared skis and lightened the sledges.

By Air, Sea, and Land

Amundsen was one of the world's greatest polar explorers. He never retired from exploring, and always found another way of approaching a geographic goal.

Back to the Arctic

Amundsen became famous for completing the Northwest Passage in 1906 and reaching the South Pole in 1911. He did not end his career in exploration after returning from Antarctica. After **World War I**, he launched other expeditions to the Arctic by sea, by airplane, and by flying blimp.

The *Maud*

Amundsen entered the shipping business, which allowed him to have a new ship built, similar in design to the *Fram*. The *Maud*, named after Norway's queen, sailed from Norway through the **Northeast Passage**, along the northern coast of Europe and Asia. The *Maud* spent the winter frozen in the ice off the northern coast of Asia. It was here that Amundsen encountered some bad luck. First, he broke his shoulder when he tripped over one of the dogs onboard and fell off the ship's gangplank into the snow. Shortly after, he was attacked by a polar bear, which had been enraged by the ship's watchdog. He might have been killed if the dog not returned to lead the bear away on another chase. He recovered from his injuries, but again was nearly killed when a lamp leaked poisonous carbon monoxide gas into the area where he was working. The voyage finally came to an end when a broken propeller forced the *Maud* to sail to Seattle, Washington, for repairs.

Amundsen built a new ship, the Maud, *in 1918 for another expedition to the North Pole.*

The British accused Amundsen of deceit for the way he had concealed his venture to Antarctica. When news of Robert Scott's death circulated, Amundsen was blamed by some for rushing Scott's team into a race before they were fully prepared. These claims ignored the fact that Scott was already in the Antarctic and his trek had been planned well in advance.

- 1903-1906 -

Amundsen sails the Northwest Passage on the *Gjoa*.

- 1910-1911 -

Amundsen heads to Antarctica in the *Fram* and treks to the South Pole.

- 1918-1925 -

Aboard the *Maud*, Amundsen attempts the Northeast Passage.

Flying over the Arctic

After the disastrous sail of the *Maud*, Amundsen was eager to try a new form of transportation in 1925. With funds from a wealthy American named Lincoln Ellsworth, Amundsen purchased two seaplanes. He and Ellsworth, along with two pilots and two other crew members, set off to explore the Arctic by air. This mission also ran into troubles, and the planes were forced to land on the ice. One of the planes was damaged and had to be left behind. Again, Amundsen narrowly escaped with his life.

People thought Amundsen's planes had been lost at sea when he returned from flying in the Arctic.

The *Norge*

Amundsen had become an explorer because of his childhood dream of visiting the North Pole. His last mission of exploration finally brought him there.

In 1926, with funding from Lincoln Ellsworth, he purchased an airship designed by Italian Umberto Nobile. He had missed out on the opportunity to be first to the North Pole, but he could still be the first to fly over it. Again, he was disappointed. Admiral Richard E. Byrd, an American aviator, made a flight across the Arctic only two days before Amundsen's airship, the *Norge*, took off. Piloted by Nobile, the *Norge* flew from the island of Spitsbergen directly across the North Pole, landing in Teller, Alaska. Amundsen released a small Norwegian flag directly over the pole.

One Final Flight

After the *Norge*'s flight, Umberto Nobile claimed credit for the polar crossing. Amundsen, who had organized the venture, was upset. A few years later, Nobile purchased his own airship, the *Italia*, and organized an all-Italian flight over the pole. The *Italia* had succeeded in its goal and was making its return flight when it disappeared. In spite of the hostility he had felt for Nobile in the past, Amundsen volunteered to lead a rescue mission. This turned out to be his final expedition. Nobile and his crew were rescued, but Amundsen's plane did not return.

(above) Amundsen flew over the North Pole in the airship Norge, *piloted by Umberto Nobile.*

(left) Amundsen died June 18, 1928, when his plane crashed while searching for the Italia. Pieces of Amundsen's wrecked plane were discovered two months later.

After Amundsen

The success of Amundsen's expedition to the South Pole opened the door to further exploration of Antarctica. It also had lasting effects on international affairs.

Trapped in Ice

After Amundsen's triumph at the South Pole, other adventurers were eager to make their mark. Ernest Shackleton led an expedition to cross the entire Antarctic continent in 1914. His ship, the *Endurance*, was crushed by pack ice in the Weddell Sea off the western coast. For six months, he and his crew were forced to camp on the ice until it finally broke up enough for them to launch their lifeboats in open water. After six days at sea in the lifeboats, they arrived at **Elephant Island**.

Amazing Escape

From there, Shackleton and five others set out on a courageous journey to find help. They landed 800 miles (1,300 kilometers) away on South Georgia island, but still had to cross a mountain range on foot to reach a whaling station on the opposite side of the island. Help was sent for the men left behind, and after several attempts to reach them through the thick ice surrounding Elephant Island, they were eventually rescued by a Chilean naval ship. Not a single man was lost.

Pole Flyer

The age of flight brought more adventure-seekers to Antarctica. Admiral Richard E. Byrd, who had flown over the Arctic in 1926, became the first man to fly over the South Pole three years later.

Admiral Byrd established the Little America base at the Bay of Whales. The base had radio towers to allow communication with the rest of the world. Many nations eventually set up research stations in Antarctica.

Whaling Revisited

Antarctic waters had long been a hunting ground for whaling vessels, but Amundsen's conquest of the pole brought an increasing number of ships to the area. Norwegian whaling companies had experienced difficulties due to depleted whale stocks in northern seas. They now profited greatly as Norway claimed rights of the waters off the Antarctic coast. The International Convention for the Regulation of Whaling was signed in 1946 in an effort to conserve whale stocks being exhausted by the industry.

Shackleton's ship, the Endurance, sinks in Antarctic waters. The crew salvaged what they could, including smaller lifeboats that they used to sail away from Antarctica. Shackleton was not the last explorer to risk his life in polar exploration.

Amundsen's Legacy

Roald Amundsen's accomplishments in scientific research and exploration have influenced and inspired many scientists and adventurers.

Leaving his Mark

Like many famous explorers, Amundsen's memory has been preserved on maps and monuments. The Amundsen Gulf, where the Arctic Ocean meets the Beaufort Sea, was named for the explorer who completed the Northwest Passage. Several features of the Antarctic landscape bear the explorer's name as well, including the Amundsen Sea off the western coast of the continent and the Amundsen Glacier. Near the south pole of the Moon, there is a large hole that has been named the Amundsen crater. The most famous of Amundsen's namesakes is the Amundsen-Scott Polar Research Station, an American base for scientific research located at the South Pole. The station is occupied year-round by researchers.

A statue of Roald Amundsen in Norway. A Norwegian frigate, or warship, also bears his name.

(above) Scientists do valuable work at polar research stations, such as studying global warming. Over 10,000 tourists a year visit Antarctica, brought there by private tour companies.

(below) Penguins stand beside a pile of used equipment and waste. The presence of people in Antarctica threatens their natural environment.

A Contribution to Science

Amundsen kept journals during his expeditions and published them to raise funds for his next adventure. These works represent a major contribution to history and science. Today, scientists from all over the world work at Antarctic research stations, researching things such as weather and **oceanography**. The Antarctic Treaty was signed in 1959 by twelve nations that claimed territory in Antarctica: Argentina, Australia, Belgium, Chile, France, Great Britain, Japan, New Zealand, Norway, Russia, South Africa, and the United States. They agreed to cooperate in scientific research and use the continent only for peaceful purposes.

Glossary

airship A massive flying machine that uses gases that are lighter than air to lift off the ground and fly

biological observations Scientific notes made from watching or observing nature such as plants and animals

captivate To hold an attraction through charm or beauty

conquest Something that has been conquered or overcome

diametrically A word that emphasizes two things that are different, or complete opposites

Elephant Island A mountainous or rocky island that is mostly covered with ice off the coast of Antarctica in the South Shetland Islands

endured Beared or tolerated hardships

exploit To use or take advantage unfairly

geological The structure of the Earth's surface features, origins, and history, and the study of rocks and resources

global warming An increase in the Earth's average temperature that causes climate change

laurels Honor and glory won for something a person has achieved

magnetic properties Having the ability or power to attract

national glory Honor or praise for or from a country

North Magnetic Pole The northern end of the geomagnetic field that surrounds Earth. Its location is continually moving northwest. The North Magnetic Pole is different from the geographic North Pole

Northeast Passage The water route between the northern coast of Europe and Asia between the Atlantic and Pacific oceans

oceanography The scientific study of the oceans

practical Useful or efficient

ration A fixed portion of food given to people in the armed services or in times when food is scarce

scurvy A disease caused by lack of vitamin C found in fresh fruits, vegetables, and meat. Symptoms include weakness, bleeding gums, and bleeding under the skin

sealer A person who hunts or harvests seals

sledges A type of sled mounted on runners and hauled by dogs or people

South Magnetic Pole The point on the Earth's surface where geomagnetic lines are directed upwards. Its location is continually moving. The South Magnetic Pole is different from the geographic South Pole

Southern Hemisphere The half of the Earth that is south of the equator

stickler Someone who feels strongly about getting something done

trekked Traveled over land or on the sea

whaling station A place on the ocean's coast where whalers butchered whales and harvested their oil and blubber

World War I An international conflict fought mostly in Europe that lasted from 1914 until 1918

Index

Printed in the U.S.A.